From the bottom of the pond:

*The forgotten art of experiencing God
in the depths of the present moment*

From the Bottom of the Pond is a profound, lucid and accessible book, full of wisdom and compassion.

Don't just pick this book up, read it and read it again. It's the best Christian book I have read in years. This is a book that will inform, delight, and teach. It needs to be heard. It has the potential to light up Christianity. This is what happens when God is happening. It's a brave book, expressing what it feels like to feel God. It shines a light on God in the midst of life, in the detail and the dirt, and it should be on every Christian's reading list.

Simon Small offers in a very accessible form a way into the spiritual quest that takes seriously the Christian contemplative tradition, as well as the explosion of interest in spiritualities of so many kinds in our time. His own experience is at the heart of the book, yet never imposed on the reader. It is a book by which, as you read it, you feel yourself nourished at the same time as you find yourself and your questions appearing on its pages.

There is an important distinction between the outer, institutional, side of religion and its inner spiritual-experiential side. The latter is the living heart of religion. This book is a very helpful account of this in its Christian form, with practical advice about the art of immediate awareness of the divine presence, and of the effects of this in life as a whole. I commend it both to church people and to the large number of non-church people who are concerned about their own contact with the Ultimate.

A heart-warming and inspiring reminder of the essence of Christian spiritual development.

This is an important book. And it is coming out at the moment when it is needed. It is written in a language that we can all understand, mainly in short sentences, each of which adds something to build up a whole as we explore a mystery that is beyond words. Some good stories help us on the way. This short and profound book is a joy to read.

From the bottom
of the pond:

The forgotten art of experiencing God
in the depths of the present moment

SIMON SMALL

BOOKS

Winchester, U.K.
New York, U.S.A.

First published by O Books, 2007
O Books is an imprint of John Hunt Publishing Ltd., The Bothy,
Deershot Lodge, Park Lane, Ropley, Hants, SO24 oBE, UK
office1@o-books.net
www.o-books.net

Distribution in:

UK and Europe
Orca Book Services
orders@orcabookservices.co.uk
Tel: 01202 665432
Fax: 01202 666219 Int. code (44)

USA and Canada
NBN
custserv@nbnbooks.com
Tel: 1 800 462 6420
Fax: 1 800 338 4550

Australia and New Zealand
Brumby Books
sales@brumbybooks.com.au
Tel: 61 3 9761 5535
Fax: 61 3 9761 7095

Far East (offices in Singapore,
Thailand, Hong Kong, Taiwan)
Pansing Distribution Pte Ltd
kemal@pansing.com
Tel: 65 6319 9939
Fax: 65 6462 5761

South Africa
Alternative Books
altbook@peterhyde.co.za
Tel: 021 447 5300
Fax: 021 447 1430

Text copyright Simon Small 2007

Design: Jim Weaver

ISBN: 978 1 84694 066 8

A CIP catalogue record for this book is available from the British Library.

Printed in the US by Maple Vail

The quote by Archbishop Michael Ramsey is taken from:
"Be still and know"; pages 13 and 105; Fount Paperbacks (London) 1982

The quote from the Gospel of Thomas is taken from:
 "The Gospel of Thomas: The Hidden sayings of Jesus"; page
23; Marvin W. Meyer; Harper Collins 1992

The words of St Anthony of Egypt are taken from:
"The Desert Fathers"; page 137; Helen Waddell; Fontana 1962

DEDICATION

"That all may awaken to the deepest beauty,
the deepest truth and the deepest love"

CONTENTS

Prologue	From the bottom of the pond	1
1	Contemplative prayer	5
2	Christian prayer	9
3	"I can't pray"	11
4	Three-fold prayer	13
	Talking	13
	Listening	15
	Being	17
5	Morning	21
6	The Christ within	25
7	Another morning	29
8	Contemplation and order	31
9	The Body of Christ	35
10	Life	39
11	Contemplation and time	45
12	Contemplation and reality	51
13	Contemplation and love	57
14	Contemplation and truth	61
15	The rocky path of contemplation	65
	Fear	66
	Depression	68
	Walking the rocky path	72
Epilogue	The Cosmic Christ	75
Postscript		79
Further study		81

PROLOGUE

From the bottom of the pond

I rest at the center of space. Unimaginably vast space everywhere I look, disappearing into the distance, seemingly without end.

I look into the night sky, aware of countless nebulae, stars and galaxies, seen and unseen. I am also aware of the darkness in which they have their being. I marvel that the light that enters my eye from each will have taken years, if not eons to complete its journey. I am seeing the universe as it was. With the farthest objects, I see the universe before the Earth was. Now and the past, present in the same moment.

I feel very small, a pinprick of consciousness filled with awe. I become very aware of the tiny lump of rock on which I stand, orbiting an insignificant sun, on the edge of a galaxy of millions of suns. As I look up, I stand at the bottom of a shallow pond – a pond not of liquid, but of gas, without which this pinprick of consciousness would within seconds be no more. My fragility is terrifying and inspiring. My life, utterly mysterious.

As outer space fills and stills the mind, a deep intuition of inner space also begins to grow. The body that watches, itself a transient composite of star-stuff, seems flea-like when set against the glories of the cosmos. Yet as it is brought into awareness, it becomes a limitless universe in itself. Unseen yet known, billions of cells, living and dying, comprise the orchestra of embodied existence, unaware of the wholeness to which they are essential. Further out into the inner universe from where I stand at the bottom of the pond, molecules break down into atoms, which in turn open to reveal a sea of space in which is set the dance of infinitesimal particles. A dance in which the dancers never touch, are separated by vast distances, yet are bound together by a force far stronger than gravity. And the dance and the dancers exist in a world where my rules do not apply. They wink in and out of existence and can be in two places at the same time. My rules do not apply, yet the dancers respond to my attention. They dance for me when I watch, but are something else when I turn away. They hint at yet more worlds and universes of which I know nothing.

I stand at the bottom of the pond as the fulcrum of limitless space, within and without. A gateway to both, an icon that joins the two. But who am I, so small and insignificant yet at the heart of existence?

As I ponder this question, infinite space reveals itself once more. For as hard as I look, I cannot find myself. I can only find thoughts, memories, fears, beliefs and concepts that constantly arise and cease. But whoever I am does not arise or cease. I am who I have always been. Different thoughts and a new body, but I am who I am. And as my mind stills, consciousness expands without limit. There is a deep sense that, indeed, it has no limit. It, too, is infinite, vibrantly alive space.

As I stand at the bottom of the pond, I am the still center of awesome space. But so is every other human being. And, in its own way, so is every animal, plant, virus, bacteria and living cell. And in some far distant galaxy, on another insignificant lump of rock, at the bottom of another pond, stands another still center of space staring upwards and inwards, filled and humbled by the Mystery of Existence.

Two thousand years ago a man came to awaken us to the Mystery of Existence. He was the Mystery made flesh, the Mystery fully aware of itself. He taught awakening in different ways to different people, for reasons only he understood. In some he nurtured the seed of contemplation that it might grow and fill their minds. He has continued to teach this down the centuries and continues to teach it today. In our age, many are ready to listen.

1

Contemplative prayer

"Be still, and know that I am God"

(PSALM 46 VERSE 10)

Contemplative prayer is the art of paying attention to what is.

To pay profound attention to reality is prayer, because to enter the depths of this moment is to encounter God. There is always only now. It is the only place that God can be found.

Our minds find paying full attention to now very difficult. This is because our minds live in time. Our thoughts are preoccupied with past and future, and the present moment is missed. This means that the reality of God is missed. We live in a dream; contemplation is waking up.

There are many forms of contemplative prayer, but they all involve bringing the mind into the present moment. It is the only goal, but not the only fruit. In the practice of contemplative prayer we wait attentively for the Now to express itself. The form this takes will always be unique and sometimes hidden. The moment when the depths of now are revealed is when contemplative prayer becomes contemplation. It is a blurred and fuzzy boundary. Often it is only in looking back that it is apparent that the boundary has been crossed. We practice contemplative prayer; contemplation is a gift from God. It is Grace and cannot be controlled.

Because our minds are addicted to thinking, they have to be trained to pay attention to reality. This is not an indictment of thinking. Thinking is necessary and good and as much a gift from God as contemplation. Both are an expression of what it is to be human. But contemplation is the root of all that is holy.

It is impossible to stop thinking through an act of will. It has the opposite effect to that desired. We know this from our own experience. Thoughts are like rubber balls; the harder we throw them away, the harder they bounce back at us. The only way is to gently lay the ball down. In contemplative prayer we do this, not by resisting thought, but by focussing it gently and with compassion. As thought becomes focussed, one-pointed, the usual chaos of the mind subsides and the present moment is experienced ever-more deeply. Sometimes, eventually, mysteriously, even the focussed experience of thought drops away and the Now of God is experienced with all its unfathomable richness.

At other times this never happens and focussing the mind seems to be impossible. Yet even this is a gift if we are prepared to explore the deep currents of thought that are keeping us out of the present moment.

There are many methods to focus thought. Repeating a word or phrase in the mind, slowly and rhythmically; holding a visualization of an image; watching the breath; or bringing awareness to different parts of the body are some of the methods used. There are others. Over time an individual may find different methods useful, but they all seek to evoke the same experience.

For a contemplative, the methods become part of a way of life. Perhaps they are practiced twice a day. Over time, gradually, the quality of our mind changes until contemplation arises in the midst of daily life and changes the world. This then reinforces the times of formal practice, which in turn deepens our experience of being alive. It is a virtuous learning circle. We have made ourselves available to see through holy eyes, by the Grace of God.

Contemplative prayer is a calling. It is not for everyone. It lies alongside, and in full communion with other forms of prayer. Contemplatives still talk to God, praise God, thank God, get angry with God, confess to God, ask God for things and try to listen to God. But the root of their prayer life is contemplation. Why some are so called is a mystery; it is an expression of the mystical body of Christ.

In the history of the Christian tradition, contemplative prayer has sometimes been prominent and sometimes hidden. In recent times it has been almost forgotten. It is something that has only happened on the edge, practiced by the few. But, for whatever reason, we live in an age in western society where large numbers of people, often without understanding the urge within them, are drawn to experience stillness and its mysteries. The Christian tradition has much to offer such seekers, whether they reside within its boundaries or beyond. This book is such an offering.

2

Christian prayer

A Christian prays. It is what we do. It is what marks us out. Prayer, even if known by another name, is what marks out all religious people. Prayer is the spiritual path.

Many people seek to live good lives. They strive to help others, to be humble and to live ethically. Admirable as this is, however, it is not in itself the spiritual path. Spirituality is about relationship, but not in the first instance relationship with other people. It is about relationship with the depths of existence, the source of all, the Mystery from which all things come and to which they return. All other relationships, whether with people or any other aspect of creation, are but expressions of this one, primal relationship.

Christians have a particular word for the great Mystery – they call it God. This is a word shared with many other religions, but Christians have a particular understanding of the nature of the relationship. It is deeply personal. They relate to God "person to person", as a child to an utterly loving parent. For a Christian, God is not some faceless, impersonal field of existence, but the ultimate expression of enlightened personhood. This is not to say that Christians limit God to personhood, for this would be to make God in our image. Personhood is but one attribute of God, for God's nature is without limit and forever creative, but we are persons and relate most easily in this way. And so God responds in this way.

The response for a Christian is Jesus. Jesus is the ultimate expression of the closest possible relationship, for Jesus is both fully God and fully human. There can be no deeper relationship than this. The two become one, yet remain two. The expression of love has become so complete that the lovers have merged. Thus Jesus becomes the Christ.

The Christian way, therefore, is to relate to God "in the name" of Jesus. This is not to invoke a label. In the ancient wisdom a name was a word that conveyed the essence, the very nature of a person. To pray in the name of Jesus is to enter into the quality of relationship that he shares with God.

This personal connection is, however, the start of the journey and not the end. Through the doorway of the personal we can, if we are drawn, move onwards into the mystery of God, which is beyond all words and concepts.

And Christians believe one more thing that is central to their life of prayer – everything is a gift. All is Grace. The very calling to pray is itself a gift. To simply be alive is a gift, therefore every other experience is gift. We can respond wisely and lovingly to the richness of the gift, or abuse or pollute that which has been given. That is free will.

The acknowledgment that all is gift is central to Christian prayer. The deepest prayer is rooted in humility.

3
"I can't pray"

"I can't pray on my own," she said.

"Not at all?" asked the priest.

"No, only when I am in Church with others. When we are asking God for things, confessing, you know, all that sort of thing."

"But you can't talk to God at home?" the priest enquired further.

"It just seems... well, not natural for me. Not that there's anything wrong with it of course, talking to God that is. It's just that I feel it's for other people to do – not for me."

"This seems to worry you."

"I feel that I'm not doing my duty, you know, that I'm not a good Christian. I've been told since I was a child that I should pray to God, but I just don't seem able to do it."

The priest paused for a while, choosing the next words carefully.

"Tell me, are there any times when you feel particularly peaceful, you know, when your mind is more still than normal?"

The woman looked slightly puzzled by the question and did not answer immediately. She stared at the ceiling for a minute or so, but then a thought seemed to occur to her.

"The washing-up," she said suddenly.

"How do you mean?" asked the priest.

"It's like this," she replied. "Our kitchen window looks out west over the fields. At the right time of year I often stand there after dinner washing the dishes, watching the sun set." The woman started to look a little embarrassed. "Well, you're going to think I'm crazy," she continued, " but often when I'm standing there it suddenly hits me how amazing everything is." She began to warm to her theme. "You know, how beautiful the light is and the shadows as they get longer. I watch the barley swaying in the fields, and all the colors, and all the birds and insects." She was clearly getting more excited as she spoke. "And sometimes, you know, it suddenly hits me that none of this has to be; that there could just be… nothing! And that it doesn't have to be so beautiful and so…," she was clearly struggling for words, "…simple and complicated. And sometimes when this is happening my mind seems to slow down and I become very still. I feel like I am part of everything, and everything is part of me. And in those moments I kind of just know that God is there. Not some old man with a white beard, but just like, you know, present." She was struggling for words again. "Like an… energy or an atmosphere, yet also like a person."

She paused and suddenly her confidence drained away. She looked very embarrassed.

"But you think that you can't pray?" asked the priest.

"Oh no," she replied, "I can't pray at all."

4
Three-fold prayer

If prayer is the expression of relationship, to reflect on the experience of relationship must be to explore the nature of prayer.

It can be helpful to see relationship as expressing itself in three ways – "talking", "listening" and "being". These are not separate or sequential but in real relationship are intertwined within an ever-unfolding dance. Sometimes one is dominant, sometimes another. It can change from moment to moment. The boundaries are often unclear and blurred, particularly with listening and being.

But to reflect on them as if they were separate can be helpful in exploring and deepening the living experience of prayer.

Talking

In talking, we share with another our thoughts, desires, feelings and emotions. We have a deep need to do this.

In a creative way, the need arises from the profound sense

that we are on a shared journey and that in expressing to each other our experiences and thoughts the boundaries between us fall away. Each journey is unique and in the sharing of what we see, the vision of all is broadened and deepened. To lower the boundaries that usually separate us is to become vulnerable. To be vulnerable is to love. To love is to experience the essential oneness of all things and to see its mystery.

In a healing way, the need to talk can arise from the impossibility of containing the chaos of our minds. This is the most common reason for talking, but both the creative and the healing ways are often entangled in the same moment. The chaos arises because psychologically we live in mind-made time. We live in imagined futures based on perceived pasts, anticipating situations and possible threats. In this false time, we play roles and project images of who we are – which we desperately want ourselves and others to believe.

This is a mad inner-world, which seems to have a life of its own, ever-intensifying. We seek escape from the whirlwind of thought in any way possible. Perhaps we dull the mind with wine, or distract it with excitement. But talking is a God-given way. Through telling another our story the pressure is relieved for a while. It is not a cure, for this kind of talking only addresses the symptom and not the cause. But in relieving the symptom (the chaotic thinking) space is created temporarily for deeper insight.

It is also important to remember that much talking is non-verbal. We express our thoughts in many ways other than words. We communicate through our bodies, through shared rituals, through the giving and receiving of gifts, through art, through music and through self-sacrifice. Often, this is the most powerful form of talking.

So the first expression of prayer is talking to God. Telling

God our story. We share with God our guilt, desires, hopes, fears, remorse, requests and thanks. In so doing, we do not deny our emotions, which we express to God with complete honesty. Tears, joy, despair and, even, anger are directed towards God. In such honesty we can sometimes surprise ourselves by what we say. This is real relationship. In telling God our story, in truth, we find peace and a new perspective. This is the first aspect of three-fold prayer – talking to God. God is our greatest friend to whom anything can be said.

In talking to God, we also nurture the ability to listen. A full mind cannot listen.

Listening

In relationship we have to learn to listen as well as to talk. Listening is more difficult. It is more difficult because much of the time we are not really listening to the other, but to ourselves. As the other person talks we listen not to them, but to our minds. We hear them only dimly through a veil of thoughts about what their words mean for us; how what they are saying relates to our desires, fears and expectations, while we rehearse our impatient response. In so doing, we do not listen properly and miss the true meaning of what is being said. As a result, much of our thought about their words is based on misunderstanding – and this is the place from which we respond. Thus is the separation and conflict of humanity caused.

We are also not good at listening because we are obsessed with words. Yet, much talking is done without words. A flower speaks to us deeply without a sound.

So the second element of three-fold prayer is listening to God.

Most of us are not that good at talking to God, but we are even worse at listening – if we ever try at all.

To listen to God, we first of all have to stop listening to ourselves. We have to offer our minds to God that our thoughts may be shaped, colored and illumined by His spirit. Listening does not involve abandoning thought, but requires that our thinking is placed on the altar of God. The traditional Christian word for the practice of listening to God is "meditation".

One of the most ancient forms of Christian meditation is "Lectio Divina", or "holy reading". In this, the mind slowly reads a passage of sacred text or other spiritual work while inviting God to use the words on the page to illumine the mind with insight and inspiration. The words become transparent to the depths that lie beyond. They become mirrors upon which the mind of God can be glimpsed. They become pointers to that which lies beyond the literal meaning of the words; to the place that lies beyond any words.

Another form of Christian meditation is to offer the imagination to God, that He may use it to teach and to inspire. We may, for example, imagine ourselves as a participant in a great biblical scene from the life of Jesus. We allow the story to unfold as it will, and the experience of such meditation can shock and surprise. We find thoughts arising that are deeply challenging, or which give new insight into some great truth, or which suggest an unexpected course of action in our outer lives.

But Christian meditation is not limited to formal practices. Any endeavour that requires that we focus our minds can nurture meditative consciousness if we offer the moment to God. Writing, art, music, listening to another person, doing the washing-up and countless other activities can become a vehicle for God's thoughts to shine in our minds.

Also, listening to God is not only an inner experience. God speaks to us through other people and through the experiences of life. This outer voice will be heard by a mind that practices inner listening.

And throughout the practice of learning to listen to God is another, related practice – discernment. Too easily we can mistake our own voice for the wisdom of God. We have to learn the difference that we may recognize both. Self-knowledge, and the testing by others of what we believe God has said to us, are essential.

So we now have the first two elements of three-fold prayer – talking and listening. But these are not primarily the subject of this book, though they must be mentioned in order to give context. It is now possible to turn to the third element of three-fold prayer – "being".

Being

My wife and I do not speak to each other for long periods of time. We can get up early in the morning, drive a long distance and not speak until we are having breakfast at our destination. But there is nothing wrong with our relationship. On the contrary, something beautiful is happening. Our relationship has reached a depth where talking and listening are no longer needed to sustain our link. Something else is growing for which the word "relationship" begins to be inadequate. "Communion" is, perhaps, a better description.

Of course, our relationship is not always at the level of communion. Talking and listening, with all their depths, are still natural and necessary. But whereas when we first met talking and listening were the predominant expressions of our love, the balance has shifted (and is still shifting) towards communion.

A friend once told me a story. He worked from home, with his wife acting as his secretary. They spent long periods of time together and were rarely apart. One day he was working in his office when he began to feel that something had changed, that something was missing. He started to feel restless and disturbed for no obvious reason. He struggled to continue working and, eventually, the feeling suddenly went away and he felt normal again. That evening he recounted the experience to his wife. It transpired that around the time he had first felt disturbed, she had remembered that she needed something from the shop. Not wishing to disturb him, she had quietly slipped-out without saying anything. On returning to the house, she had entered as quietly as she could. Her return coincided with the easing of my friend's sense of disturbance. The experience had revealed to him just how close their relationship had become. They were joined in a way that was beyond talking, listening or even physical proximity. To some degree the two had become one.

This is relationship as "being" – as a living experience; as though two liquids or fields of energy have merged into each other, but are both still present.

It is this experience of relationship, which may be called "being" or "communion", which constitutes the third strand of three-fold prayer. It is the subject of this book. Traditionally, it has been called "contemplation". It is about being with God, fully and without distraction. It is when the two become one, through Grace.

It is not superhuman, exotic or reserved only for great saints. The experience is something we all have tasted. We have all had moments when an experience of nature, or a baby's smile, or a piece of music or an encounter with death has produced in us, at least for a few moments, a profound stillness and a sense of oneness with everything, allied to a conviction that all is well. These are timeless moments. They are a taste of being with God. We return to the everyday world inspired and renewed. We have glimpsed the root of all religion.

Contemplative prayer is the practice of making ourselves available for such communion, should it be the will of God.

5
Morning

The mind does not want to still. It is now getting light and the cup of coffee has been finished. There is a temptation to pick up the cup once more just in case there are a few drops left – anything to put off the effort of bringing stillness to the mind. Thought clamours. From the moment of awakening, the mind has been convinced there is a problem that requires urgent attention. It does not know what the problem is, but it must exist. Since that moment the mind has accelerated, as it has begun the process of obsessing with the challenges of the day ahead. Perhaps one of them is "the" problem.

The contemplative knows that unless the commitment to stilling is made as soon as possible, the mind will begin to resemble wild horses racing around a paddock. It is better to calm the horses now, rather than later when it will be much more difficult.

The contemplative sits upright in the chair, closes her eyes, uncrosses her legs and rests her hands in her lap, one gently lying on the other, palms upward. Experience has shown that, mysteriously, a balanced and ordered body helps bring order to the mind. Also, as the mind begins to still, in turn, the body finds that it can only hold itself in a balanced and ordered way.

Immediately the turbulence of the mind diminishes. It was so simple. Yet why was the resistance so great?

She begins to focus attention on the sounds around her. The ticking of the clock, the distant rumble of traffic, an occasional bird, the murmur of the heating system. The mind is not manufacturing anything – it is simply paying close attention to what is, to the reality of the moment. Inevitably from time to time the mind wanders and extraneous thoughts intrude. The contemplative has learned through experience that this does not matter. Her attention is simply refocused on the sounds that are present in the moment. If the intruding thoughts are seen as a problem, they will be fought. A conflicted mind cannot find stillness. All that is needed is to refocus on what is. Thoughts are not real.

She has learned, and is still learning, to listen to sound in a new and profound way. The mind is deeply conditioned to judge and to label every experience, and from this arises the endless commentary that fills our heads. In contemplative prayer, the practice is to lay aside this conditioning and to experience reality without labelling it good, bad or whatever. So, as the contemplative listens, she practices acceptance of every sound, being at peace with it, as it is. No inner choice is made between the revving engine and the bird singing. Both are listened to without inner comment. No labels are attached. After a while, sometimes, the practice of acceptance can lead to an astonishing experience. Every sound becomes a wonderful, subtle music. The revving engine has its own beauty, every bit as great as the bird song. It is as though she has connected with the deeper rhythms of creation, which permeate all experience.

After a few minutes, the contemplative gently moves attention away from the surrounding sounds and begins to focus on the body. At first, attention is given to the body as a whole; to the feeling of being a body, a construct of bone and flesh. The contemplative becomes aware of the subtle sense of "aliveness" that permeates every part of the body, like a delicate vibration. The mind begins to fill with a deep wonder at the very extraordinariness of being a body. We miss the astonishing reality of being alive in a body through the ferment of our thinking and the busyness of our living. When we remember we are alive, something extraordinary happens.

The contemplative then begins to refine her attention to focus on particular parts of the body. Perhaps a start is made at the feet. Her attention is first of all allowed to rest in one foot and all the subtle sensations, always present but usually missed, arise into consciousness. Then the attention is allowed to slowly ascend to the top of the leg, before being gently refocused on the other foot and the experience repeated. After this, the focussed attention is allowed to rise slowly upwards through the body, being conscious of each part encountered and all the sensations that it offers. Finally, she is simply present in that mysterious space behind the eyes where "I" seems to live.

And there is stillness.

There are thoughts passing across the mind, arising and ceasing. There are sensations in the body, arising and ceasing. But the contemplative has become the vibrantly alive stillness that embraces and enables all that arises and ceases. She has become the timeless through which time passes.

And the contemplative spends some time in the timeless. She becomes aware that she is not alone. There is some indefinable boundary where she ends and something greater continues. She is not the greater, but the greater is her. She is experiencing relationship of such profound depth that the lovers, while still two, are in the same moment fully one. The greater has individuality, purpose and vast intelligence, but is also so much more than she can understand.

In this place, a new kind of thought occasionally arises. It is not like the usual mish-mash of thoughts that fill the head, which are still there vaguely in the background. The new thoughts are of a different quality. They arise from the stillness and reflect its light. They are thoughts that in the days to come will evoke stillness and insight in the midst of the world.

After a while, the flow of creation gradually leads the contemplative away from the depths of stillness, back into the world of form and time. There is nothing wrong with this; it is where she is meant to be for now. But she is reluctant to come back. Where once there was resistance to entering the stillness, there is now resistance to leaving it. Contemplation, however, is not about escaping from the world; it is about nurturing a new relationship with life, so that one can truly love God and one's neighbor.

Slowly the mind fills once more with the world, until the moment comes when her eyes open of their own accord and to stretch seems wonderful.

The sound of mail falling through the letterbox intrudes. Time to engage with the world.

6

The Christi within

"On that day you will know that I am in
my Father, and you in me, and I in you."
(GOSPEL OF JOHN CHAPTER 14 VERSE 20)

A single beam of sunlight shines through a pane of glass and strikes an ancient stone floor. Its brightness and clarity contrast wonderfully with the murky interior of the building. A small area of a stone slab is illumined and every detail, no matter how tiny, is picked out with breath-taking precision. Every grain of dust and the texture of the stone, with its unevenness where it has been worn away by countless feet, can be seen effortlessly.

In that patch of light is something unique. Nowhere else in the universe will an identical collection of shapes, colors and textures be found. Something utterly individual has been created by the beam of light, yet in the same moment the small area of stone is still one with the rest of the material universe. It is both the whole and an individual.

And something even more profound is happening. It is

a question of identity. "Who" is that unique expression of individuality – is it the stone or the light? At one level it is both, in that the creation of uniqueness arises out of the relationship of the two. But it is the light, the Sun, that came first, that initiated the moment of creation.

In that moment the Sun became the unique patch of stone, but the patch of stone can never be the Sun.

Sooner or later, contemplation leads us to the fundamental spiritual question – "Who am I?" It leads us, very disturbingly, to the realization that this question cannot be answered.

When we pay attention to the present moment, without commentary or judgement, to both the inner and outer worlds, the mind begins to still. Space appears around and between thought. We discover in the stillness that we are not our thoughts, we are the thinker. We are the space in which thoughts come and go.

But for most of our lives our sense of identity, of who we are, has been based on our thoughts. Our name, history, beliefs, likes and dislikes, ambitions and thoughts about how we wish others to regard us, have combined into a thought picture of an "individual" whom we have been convinced that we are. We have confused ourselves with our thoughts.

In the stillness of contemplation, however, we take a step back from thought and are surprised to discover that we do not die; indeed, we experience life in its fulness. It is an awakening from a dream of identity, like an actor suddenly remembering that they are not the character being played. We are still present, manifest in this world, but no longer intoxicated by it.

As we rest for a while in the stillness, in that space in which thoughts are born, live and die, strangely there is still a profound sense of being "someone", of being a unique individual. However, no words will suffice to contain this experience of personhood.

There is just an experience of intensely alive "presence". This is who we truly are. We are the child of the light and the stone; the fruit of that relationship.

And in that stillness, there is a profound knowing that all is alive and that life is infinite and eternal; that this particular, individual expression of presence arises from something immeasurably greater; that there is me and a transcendent "other", between whom there is both a boundary and a oneness, and that this "other" is intensely alive, intelligent and loving. The other is also individual in a way beyond words, but also more than individual.

This "other" is the Christ within. It is the promise of Jesus fulfilled.

7
Another morning

The contemplative finishes her coffee, uncrosses her legs, sits upright and begins to still her mind. This morning she is determined to succeed. For several days her attempts at entering into contemplation have been frustrating and disturbing. No matter how much she has tried to pay attention to her point of focus, her mind has been unable to still. Within a short time she has been distracted by a torrent of thoughts and emotions. But this morning she is not going to accept her weakness and will hold her attention focussed no matter what.

Within a couple of minutes her eyes are open again. She feels like giving-up completely. If it were possible, her mind is worse today than it was yesterday. It seems that no act of will can force it to be still.

In her anger and frustration she begins to rail against God. Why isn't He helping? If she is called to practice contemplative prayer, why is it so difficult? Why is the world such a nasty place and life such a struggle?

The complaints, full of anger and resentment, pour out. A

part of her watches in horror and amazement. Can it really be right to talk to God in this way? And where is all this venom coming from? She never knew it was there.

But it feels good and it feels liberating. It is as though a great pressure is easing.

As she watches the great torrent of prayer, it starts to change and become more focussed. She finds herself telling God about a particular situation in her life. She is surprised to discover just how worried she is about it. She never realized.

Eventually, she finishes talking to God. All that needed to be said, has been said. She feels drained, a bit embarrassed, but wonderfully lightened, as though she has laid down a great weight that she has been carrying for a long time without realizing.

She gathers herself. She now knows why she could not enter into the stillness. There was something that needed to be shared with God with honesty and emotion. It has now been said, so it is time to listen. She sits upright once more, closes her eyes and asks for God's guidance.

This time she enters the stillness without effort. She finds herself listening with rapture to the sounds around her. Her attention moves after a while to her body and she becomes acutely aware of each part in turn. Then, with wonderful power, her mind is filled with the astonishment of simply being alive; of being here, now. She is aware of the beautiful mystery of everything and, somehow, in the experience of that mystery her prayer is answered. She does not know the answer yet, but the seed has been planted and will mature. It will be encountered in due time in her mind or in the world.

And the answer to her prayer will be rooted on one great truth – she is never alone.

8

Contemplation and order

Contemplation is the art of paying profound attention to what is. It is a radically different state of consciousness from that normally experienced by human beings. The non-contemplative mind is scattered, fragmented and lost in imagination, as it searches amidst myriad thoughts for peace and security.

A contemplative mind, being not scattered, fragmented or lost in unreality, is therefore an ordered mind. This is not a manufactured order imposed by strength of will, but an order that naturally arises from being connected with reality. It is an order rooted in simplicity, for the real is simple. It is an order rooted in acceptance, for to deny what is real is madness. And from this state of acceptance arises the wisdom not to manufacture unnecessary choice.

A contemplative mind is rooted in the present moment, which is perfectly harmonized for it is an expression of a perfect universe. From this rooted stillness, a contemplative mind expands into creative action as and when the flow of life so requires, bringing full attention to bear on each action.

A contemplative mind has been described, with deceptive simplicity, as a mind that just does the next thing that needs to be done.

An ordered mind inevitably out-pictures into an ordered life; a life of focus, concentration and gentle rhythm. But it is a two-way street, for if an ordered mind leads to an ordered life, so must an ordered life nurture contemplative consciousness. Thus in the Christian tradition, and in many others, great importance is placed on living according to a "rule of life", which reinforces and is reinforced by other spiritual practices associated with contemplation.

Each day will be lived around certain landmarks. There will be, perhaps, a time for prayer, a time for work, a time for spiritual reading, a time for play and a time to rejoice in the company of those we love. There will also be a commitment to living life as slowly as we can. It is impossible to pay profound attention while living at a frenzied pace. Of course, we all come to the contemplative path at different stages of life, in different conditions and with different commitments. So, beginning to live an ordered life must be a gradual process, accepting with good grace the limitations of our current life situation. But, over time, the aspiration to introduce order will result in different decisions being made from what would have previously been the case.

For many in our present-day society there is great inner resistance to living an ordered life. Chaos is confused with freedom; order with restriction and imprisonment. What is not understood is that the opposite is true. Order is not a denial of freedom, but a great liberation. For order unleashes the vast amount of energy previously dissipated and wasted through chaotic and fragmented living. Order focuses and concentrates and thereby gives birth to astonishing creative power – and to be creative and to be free are one and the same thing.

And order has another great gift, which is often not recognized – an ordered life is deeply compassionate. It is compassionate in that as a mind grows into contemplation, it naturally affects and heals other minds with whom it comes into contact. It is also compassionate in a more worldly sense, the value of which should not be underestimated. To be late for meetings, to forget promises, not to pay bills on time, not to complete agreed work and to be generally unreliable is to be deeply unkind to other people. It is not an intended unkindness, for it arises out of unconsciousness, but it is unkind nevertheless.

It can be a great shock to a disordered person to realize this and can trigger remorse and guilt. But this moment is also an opportunity. For the realization of how unkind one has been can provide great motivation and energy for finally overcoming the inner resistance to living an ordered life. And through this great act of kindness to others, one's own life is transformed.

We have given and received. We are learning how to love our neighbor.

9
The Body of Christ

For just as the body is one and has many members,
and all the members of the body, though many, are
one body, so it is with Christ... If the whole body
were an eye, where would the hearing be? If the whole
body were hearing, where would the sense of smell be?

We have been given the gift of individuality. We are not called to be all the same. Indeed, in the Christian tradition this diversity is celebrated and recognized as a fundamental characteristic of creation. The flow of creation is an expansion from oneness to multiplicity, from uniformity to variety. Yet, this is not a random individuality, for each part is an essential element of a wholeness – and it is the whole which gives each part its true meaning.

Imagine an orchestra made up of many different kinds of musical instruments. An orchestra comprising only violins or clarinets would be incapable of all but the simplest music.

A great symphony requires the different instruments of the orchestra to be different, fully, without holding back. It requires the musicians to bring their unique talents to bear in the service of the whole. Uniqueness and difference are shaped into something greater than the sum of the parts, by the music and the conductor.

So it is with the spiritual life. Each of us is called to make a unique contribution to the unfolding of God's creation. As we accept this calling, we become co-creators in God. We can surprise God. Unfortunately, however, whilst we may accept the importance of difference at an intellectual level, most of us have great difficulty in real life. The human mind tends to be absolutist by nature. It is very drawn to assert that there is only one way, which usually translates as "my way". The issue frequently arises in the relationship between contemplation and other expressions of Christianity.

For many Christians their faith is about making the world a better place through action. It is about alleviating suffering, helping the poor, peace-making and the cultivation of justice. It is about ritual, ceremony and words. It is about looking away from oneself into the world. There are wonderful examples throughout history and in the present day where this expression of Christianity has achieved marvellous things in the world. This calling is holy and clearly of God.

But it can be difficult for such Christians, who tend to be the large majority, to appreciate and accept the way of those drawn to the inner path. For them, a life centered around stillness and silence can appear self-centered and uncaring. People drawn to the contemplative life can find it hard to live in such an atmosphere. Indeed, it may cause them to question their vocation. It can seem easier to live a contemplative life outside mainstream Christian community.

All of us need to remember and reflect upon the words of St Paul with which this chapter began. We need to remember that the instrument of the orchestra that only sounds occasionally is just as important as the rest. We need to remember that without the silence all music is meaningless. We need to remember that music arises from silence and returns to silence. We need to remember that each note of music is surrounded by silence and, without it, would be nothing.

10
Life

"I came that they may have life,
and have it abundantly."

(GOSPEL OF JOHN CHAPTER 10 VERSE 10)

Something extraordinary happens when we become aware of being alive.

Try it now.

Become aware of your own presence in this moment. As you hold this book, become conscious of holding the book. You are here and it is there. Notice the texture of the paper and the contrast with the ink. Become sensitive to the feel of the book in your hands, on your fingertips and on your palms.

As you do this, be aware of the rhythm of your breathing, the gentle rise and fall of your chest and that very subtle, delicate vibration of the body that we call life. Notice the experience of sitting and any surrounding sounds. Without striving, allow your awareness to continue to expand.

After a while, ask yourself a question. The question might

be, "What am I?" or "What is life?" or "Why is there anything?" Choose the question that seems to evoke something within you. But, very importantly, make no attempt to answer the question. Simply allow it to lie gently on your mind, as a piece of driftwood floats on a gentle sea.

It may be that a deep feeling of the unutterable mystery of existence will arise within.

Stay in this place for a few minutes.

* * *

Actually, this quality of awareness is not extraordinary at all; it just seems that way. It is simply the rediscovery of reality and, if we are honest, there can be nothing extraordinary about reality. It is what it is; it is the way it is, with nothing added and nothing taken away. It is truth. Not *this* truth or *that* truth, but truth in its wholeness. It is impossible to become profoundly aware of being alive and not enter deeply into this moment, to discover a wealth that was always present but only occasionally glimpsed. This moment is all that there is and so this moment is the truth.

It is in opening to the awareness of the astonishing fact of our own existence that true peace is found. Our relationship with everything and everyone is transformed. This happens because when we become aware of being alive, it becomes self-evident that we are just a unique expression of something so great that it is beyond imagination. When we truly become aware of being alive, we stop taking life too personally.

When we stop taking life too personally, something else happens. The barriers that we have erected in our minds between life and us fall away. We realize that we are life and life is us, and it was never any different except in the fantasies of our thoughts. We no longer feel the need to be special. The existential sense of loneliness, of being cut-off, that has lain in the depths of each of us for so long, is healed. Life is no longer an enemy to be fought, but exultant being.

We experience life in its fulness.

"God" becomes more than just a word.

There have been moments in the past when we have spontaneously tasted life in its fulness. For many this will have been when close to nature – a walk through a forest with sunbeams penetrating the canopy, creating a wonderful contrast of light and shade; the view from a mountain top; or, perhaps, a bubbling stream with myriad patterns of reflection. Another person might have evoked in us the fulness of life for a few minutes – a baby's smile, or the sight of an artist at work. Sometimes the experience arises when we have lost ourselves in creative activity, whether it is playing a piece of music, painting a picture, repairing a leaking pipe, or washing the dishes.

The unutterable mystery of our own life can also hit us around birth and death. To see a baby born, or to deeply ponder its evolution in the womb can shake us to our core. The death of someone we know, particularly if we were present when they died, can remind us forcefully of the impermanence of our own body; that there was a time before we were and that time will continue after we are gone. Perhaps we suddenly see our "life" as the brief spark that it actually is.

Such moments always take us by surprise. They are revealed, not manufactured. There is always the sense of "losing oneself" into a "timeless" moment. It is like a profound awakening. It is a profound awakening. We never forget such moments. They are moments of contemplation.

For most of us, the experience never lasts more than a short while. The mind kicks-in and we re-enter time and ourselves.

We fall asleep again and dream the world of the human mind.

Imagine what would happen if we could live from the consciousness of awakened life all of the time, in the midst of the everyday world.

Most of the time, though, we are not aware of being alive. We are too busy living. Our daily dramas, plans and desires fill our minds. We are addicted storytellers (both waking and sleeping), constantly rehearsing scripts and scenarios that we wish to arise or that may arise. The more mental energy we give our stories, the faster they spin and the more intense the experience becomes. It is powerfully addictive and feeds on itself. It is the ultimate drug and, like any drug, increasing amounts are needed to maintain the intensity. Should the intensity drop for any length of time, we believe that something has gone wrong.

This is a dream world that we confuse with reality. We seek peace, contentment and happiness in illusion. As one fantasy fails to satisfy (a discovery that can take minutes or decades) we seek another. If we run out of fantasies to pursue, we say that life has become meaningless.

It does not occur to us to awaken from our dreams of life and discover life itself. By its very nature, the reality of life is always fulfilling. But life is only to be found now. Our dramas, plans and desires take our awareness out of this moment into time. We believe that this moment is not good enough, not complete, and can be bettered, so we try to imagine the "perfect moment". If we still have hope, our awareness is focussed on the future. If hope has gone, we focus on the past. "Anywhere but now!" is our cry

When we become aware of being alive we find peace. It is a peace which flows from the heart of existence itself. It is a peace that is vibrantly intelligent, loving and creative. In the

Christian tradition we call it the peace of God. It is not a peace dependent upon outward circumstances or even how we feel. It is the peace of the deep. Storms may rage on the surface, but our anchor rests in the stillness of the depths.

It is so simple. But it is its simplicity that defeats us. Our time-bound minds tell us that answers are found in complexity, not simplicity.

In a way, it is alchemy. It is from that most base of substances, life itself, that gold is revealed.

11

Contemplation and time

We only become aware of life when we are still. Stillness, in turn, generates awareness of being alive.

By this is meant inner stillness. Outer stillness is very helpful in nurturing this experience, but ultimately is not essential. Otherwise, living in the everyday world would become very difficult.

The problem is that deep within us, so deep that we are not usually aware of it, our minds experience an ever-present "tug to the next moment". It is so subtle, yet powerfully cuts us off from the beauty of life. The tug can be pleasurable anticipation or dread, but either way it takes our awareness into the illusion of the next moment. We cease to be alive.

I was once asked by a friend to help him go more deeply into life. He had worked hard for many years and lived very actively. The "tug to the next moment" was very evident in him. One day we decided to go to a local beauty spot for a walk. As we pulled into the car park, I saw how I might be able to show him "the tug" in all its persuasiveness. The moment we got out of the car, he was ready to march off. The sun was shining and the hills beckoned. It was the tug of pleasurable anticipation.

But when we reached the edge of the car park, I stopped and suggested that we go no further for the time being.

Before us was a path that led around the bottom of a hill and turned out of sight a little way ahead. We stopped and went no further. I suggested that we observe ourselves for a while and see what we could learn. Within seconds we felt the tug to the next moment become apparent. Something deep within us objected to simply standing still – it wanted to go around that corner that lay just before us on the path. We began to sense how the "tug" was rooted in a belief that what was around the corner might be better than "this". Simply standing still started to reveal how, in our depths, we were always looking for a better moment than this. The power of the tug was, for a while, almost overwhelming.

Yet, we both knew that should we walk around that corner, the tug would still be there and we would then have to go around the next turn, then over the hill in front, and so on, never being satisfied. As we stood there, we noticed how many people marched past us, heads down (when they were not talking to each other) perversely satisfied that there was an endless supply of corners ahead.

We endured the tug and did not give in to it and, after a while, our consciousness began to change. Very gradually, we began to be acutely aware of our surroundings and the moment we were in. We first of all noticed the trees going away from the edge of the car park into a shallow valley. It was early autumn and the air was crystal clear. The play of light on the leaves began to transfix us and we noticed how wonderful was the green of the ferns between the trees. Each breath of air began to be appreciated. So too, the touch of the slight breeze on the skin. Even the car park itself (and this really was a miracle) began to have a strange beauty.

Finally, we noticed something else. The tug to the next moment, to walk around the bend in the path, was gone. That moment on the edge of the car park had become eternal, or, rather, the ever-present eternal was revealed. Even now, the memory of the experience has an astonishing clarity.

Eventually, we did walk around the bend in the path; not through discontent with where we were, but simply because it became the thing to do.

The tug to the next moment can also take the form of dread. Our minds can become preoccupied with the fear of what the future may bring. We can all think of many experiences in our lives which illustrate this fact. We will, in some way, all be experiencing the tug of dread about something in our futures as these words are read. A difficult meeting tomorrow, financial worries, a relationship going sour, illness or thoughts of our death – the examples are easy to find.

But, strangely, the power of the tug can most clearly be seen in "little" things. I have begun to notice the tug of dread when there is some empty time ahead of me. I do not know what to do next. This can happen in the morning upon awakening when I have a clear day. I have noticed how my mind immediately begins to accelerate as it searches for ways to fill the time. The sense of relief when it thinks of something to do is palpable. I have noticed it also when I come home from work in the evening. I have two hours until there is something on the television that I might want to watch – my mind begins to feel very strange.

The tug to the next moment dominates our lives. It is what cuts us off from the fulness of life. Its power comes from its hidden nature. When we become still – usually first outwardly, then inwardly – its hiding place is revealed. In the light of awareness it will fight energetically for a while, but will always eventually succumb.

It is then that the fulness of life is rediscovered.

In the fulness of life a new relationship with the next moment is revealed. The next moment is not denied, but it is known from inner stillness. My friend and I did eventually walk around the bend in the path, but it was not in response to the tug. The natural flow of life brought the bend in the path through us; we remained still.

From this inner timelessness it is still possible, and necessary, to operate within clock time. The earth does not cease to move around the Sun. The seasons pass. We have to plan journeys, meals and how to pay the bills – but the desperate tug to the next moment, deep in our minds, is no more. We plan no more than is necessary to live in a universe of space-time, then we return to inner stillness.

Into this inner stillness, the world will bring triumph and disaster, pleasure and pain – but our awareness of the majestic, eternal fulness of life will be the backdrop against which all such passing conditions will be seen.

To become aware of being alive is to discover the meaning of life. It was there all the time, but we were looking in the wrong place.

We searched for the meaning of life in the future. It was to be when the perfect moment arrived. Or, we believed the meaning of life would be revealed in the perfect philosophy or formula (to be discovered in the future, of course) and we would be able to exclaim, " Ah, yes, that is it!"

Or perhaps, through disillusionment, we gave up on the meaning of life – it did not exist. Meaninglessness was the meaning of life. Life's only purpose was to maximise pleasure and put off pain for as long as possible.

When one becomes aware of the mystery of one's own existence, however, the meaning of life is revealed – it is simply to be fully alive. Paradoxically, in the fulness of life the question of meaning does not even arise. The experience is so rich, so all-consuming that the question is irrelevant. A person does not ponder the meaning of life when she is fully alive.

Through the practice of close attention this can be seen. Questions of meaning disappear when inner stillness is present and reappear when the tug to the next moment reasserts itself.

12

Contemplation and reality

There was once a man lost in a thick forest at night. The forest was vast and confusing with few landmarks. Eventually the man grew weary of his aimless wandering and decided to climb a tree. Perhaps from the top he would be able to see a path out of the forest.

After a long and difficult climb, he finally reached the top of a tall tree. At first he could see nothing but the dark sky overhead, the moon and stars obscured by thick cloud, and the dark mass of trees just visible below him through the murk. As his eyes adjusted, however, he began to make out a glimmer of light in the distance and, with a surge of relief, realized that it was a cottage on a small hill in the middle of the forest. After taking a careful bearing, he climbed down the tree and began walking towards the cottage. It was a long walk and several times he lost his way and had to climb another tree. Eventually, however, he began to feel the ground rising beneath his feet and he knew that the cottage could not be too far ahead.

His pace quickened, reinvigorated by the thought of finally

reaching his destination. In his elated state, he began to imagine what he would find. He imagined emerging from the trees to find an ancient, thatched cottage with light blazing from the windows and smoke curling lazily from the chimney. In his mind's eye he sees himself knocking on a gnarled wooden door which, after a short wait, is opened by a large bearded man who gives him a warm welcome and invites him inside. The interior of the cottage is warm and cosy and the owner bids him sit by the fire while food is prepared.

As he continued to walk through the forest, in his mind's eye the man is sitting in the chair before the fire, listening to the sounds coming from the kitchen. By now he is totally absorbed in his imagination and before long is being called to the dinner table. There he discovers, to his surprise and slight consternation, that the large man does not live alone. Sitting at the table with him is a beautiful young woman. She is, the man explains, his daughter. He tells, with a tear in his eye, how her mother died many years before and how he has raised her on his own, there, in the middle of the forest where she is safe.

After an initial period of mutual shyness, the lost man and the daughter begin to get on well and soon laughter is ringing around the table. It is a wonderful meal which goes on for many hours, but eventually the lost man finds his exertions catching-up with him and he asks to be excused that he might rest. The father and daughter spring into action. He goes to prepare a bed for the lost man, while she prepares a hot bath for him. As she leaves the lost man at the door of the bathroom, she shyly points towards a door opposite which, she explains, is his bedroom. Wishing him goodnight with a warm smile, she disappears down the corridor.

In the real world, the lost man continued to plod through the forest. By now occasional glimmers of light from the cottage could be glimpsed through the trees. But the man did not see them for he was lost in his fantasy. In his mind's eye he is now in a warm bed in the stillness of the cottage, drifting off to sleep. Suddenly the silence is broken by a small sound. It is a sound he has been half-expecting. The door to his bedroom quietly opens and in the dim light he sees the beautiful daughter enter the room. Without a word she slips into bed beside him.

The man's pace through the forest quickened and he was almost running towards the light of the cottage. But he saw nothing except his fantasy.

Lost in his imagination, as well as in the forest, the man suddenly wakes up in bed. The beautiful daughter is still asleep beside him and it is another sound that has caused his awakening. There is movement outside the bedroom door. Before he can think what it could be, the door is flung open and light fills the room. The girl is startled awake and screams, as she sees her father standing in the doorway, a murderous face complimented by a large knife in his hand. But it is not her whom he is looking at, but at the man in bed beside her.

In his imagination, which has now become his reality, he leaps from the bed and ducks beneath a huge swing of the knife. The father is off-balance for a moment and the man seizes the opportunity to dive through the open doorway. Naked, he flies down the stairs, wrenches the cottage door open and flees into the forest, pursued by shouts and curses.

In the real forest, still lost in his imagination, the man is now running through the trees towards the cottage. Suddenly, without warning, he emerges from the trees and skids to a halt outside the door. He stares at it, transfixed for a few moments, breathing heavily. Then, with a look of absolute fury on his face, he pounds on the door until it eventually opens. There stands a small, frightened, kindly old gentleman with a pair of battered spectacles balanced precariously on the end of his nose. But this is not what the lost man sees. His fantasy has become his reality.

He presses his face close to that of the old gentleman and yells, "You can keep your so-called hospitality. And as for your daughter, I wouldn't go near her if you paid me!"

And with one final, furious stare he stomps back into the forest.

* * *

I can no longer remember when and where I first heard this story. Nevertheless, over the years it has come to mean more and more to me. It uses exaggeration and humour to convey profound insights.

Its fundamental suggestion is simple, but shocking. Most of us, most of the time, are just like the man lost in his imagination. Also, just like him, we are responding to the real world from this realm of fantasy, not from the realm of truth. As a consequence we create, needlessly, immeasurable suffering and chaos. This is bad enough at an individual level. As a collective nightmare it brings war, genocide, poverty and ecological disaster.

There is nothing esoteric about this teaching. We can see its truth simply by paying attention to our own lives.

Perhaps we have to do something that frightens us. Our mind races for hours or even days beforehand. So intense is our anticipation and rehearsal that when the moment comes we are present in body, but not in mind. Things rarely go well in such a state.

Maybe we have to discuss something difficult with another person. We dread the conversation. Our mind rehearses relentlessly in advance. We cannot sleep properly and our mind, at times, seems out of control. When the moment comes we blurt out our much-edited script. Unfortunately, the other person says something unexpected and we cannot respond because our mind is too full.

More subtly, we meet someone with a different colored skin. But we encounter them through a veil of beliefs, imaginings and prejudices. Truly, we do not meet them, but an aspect of our own minds.

There is nothing wrong in itself with imagining the future. It is a survival trait which has evolved to help us thrive and has its place. The problem is that it has become an all-absorbing, unseen addiction. We spend our time injecting ourselves with fantasy, which then becomes our reality.

This psychological process has tremendous power because it is unconscious. We do not realize what is happening. Once seen, we begin the long process of laying it down. This is not easy because it is so deeply rooted within us. Great patience and dedication are required. Over time, the process becomes easier as we make a great discovery – much of our fear was generated by our absorption in the imagination. As we return to reality, so does our experience of fear diminish. This blessing cannot be confined just to ourselves, for much of the suffering that human beings inflict upon one another is rooted in fear. As the fear is laid aside, so we become gentler, more loving people.

Contemplative prayer is giving profound attention to what is real, not what is unreal. Stilling the mind as a regular practice reveals the addiction. The more it is seen, the more its power is reduced. In stillness we observe its workings. Through contemplative practice we do not discard the imagination, for it is a great gift, but allow it to be a wonderful tool in the toolbox of wise living. We stop believing it is who we are.

13

Contemplation and love

It is in the depths of contemplation that love is discovered. Not the idea of love, beliefs about love or fantasy love, but love itself. Love has always been present, but unseen. It is not of this world, but can erupt into this world through us. Love is not an action, but action can be the fruit of love. Love, real love, is beyond words and concepts. It can only be tasted. It is to be found at the heart of now, but only when one gives profound attention to what is.

The house stood on a corner, at the junction of two roads. It was not only a meeting place for roads, but also for young people. They would gather on the broad grass verge most evenings. The excitement would mount as they competed to be more outrageous than the next. The shouting would get louder, the language more coarse and the vandalism would start. Only the public telephone box was safe from attack; it was needed to order their drugs.

The occupant of the house dreaded the summer months with their long evenings, for this was when the problem was at its worst. Day by day the anger and frustration within him would grow. Confrontation did not work. Parents and police did not seem to care.

But he was someone who prayed and, very occasionally, he listened. One evening he felt God say "watch". It was not a spoken word that was heard, but more a moment of inner clarity that could not be ignored. Perhaps he listened this time because his own answers had failed and despair was closing in. He could have listened before, but until now he had been too full of himself. The Christian tradition would call this wordless voice the Holy Spirit.

So the man who prayed positioned a chair behind the thick net curtains and began to watch. He could see, but could not be seen.

The first thing he watched, however, was not the scene in front of him, but his own mind. He observed all the thoughts of anger and injustice that bombarded his consciousness and he allowed them to be. They were not wrong and deserved acknowledgement, but tonight he was not going to become them. Then he gently moved his attention to his body and for a while became aware of each part in turn. Finally, he opened his mind to the very experience of being alive; a vibrant, mysterious patch of consciousness in the world. He marvelled at this fact. His mind became very still.

Then, with a wordless prayer that he might truly see, he opened his eyes and began to pay attention to the scene in front of him. He had looked upon it many times before but had never really seen it. He had only ever seen his own mind, he now realized. He had only seen his own fear and anger about that milling, shouting, threatening crowd. Now, gradually, from a still mind, the truth was revealed. It was fascinating.

Whereas before he had seen aggressive, strutting, loud young people, now he saw their uncertainty, their fear, their desperate need to be accepted by the group. He saw how they competed with each other for the attention of the opposite sex; how they constantly watched everyone else for signals as to how they were being viewed; how they looked at every car that passed to make sure that their outrageous behaviour had been noticed. As he watched, memories of his own adolescence came to mind.

And, slowly, compassion arose. Not the idea of compassion, but that vast spaciousness of love to which the word can only point. All the thoughts of fear, anger and condemnation were still present, but now they were but pinpricks in a majestic, wonderful background. Before they had been everything; all that he thought he was. Now he was the limitless space in which they were held. He had paid attention and seen the truth.

After a while he found his attention being drawn to one particular lad, about thirteen years old. The boy had a subtly different energy to him compared with the others. A dark, disturbed aura seemed to surround him. The man who prayed watched as the behaviour of the lad became increasingly extreme, the language more foul and the shouting more loud. He watched as the young man eventually began to attack a road sign, becoming more and more frustrated as it resisted his ministrations.

Before, what he was watching would have enraged the man who prayed. But tonight was different. In the stillness of his mind, as he paid attention, he saw in the lad's face something that touched his heart. Beneath the violence and the anger, there was great pain. Everything that was happening was rooted in that pain. The man who prayed did not see the "idea" of pain; did not imagine he saw it because a book on psychology told him that he should. He saw the pain directly, in an explosion of realization. He felt the pain.

As he continued to watch, astonishingly, the man who prayed became glad that the boy was attacking the road sign. He knew, in a way he did not understand, that the lad's pain was so great that it had to have an outlet. If the victim had not been the road sign, it would have been someone else, or the boy himself.

As the sky darkened and the crowd began to disperse, the man who prayed realized that he had rarely felt as much love for anyone as he did in that moment for that boy – as he continued to vandalize the road sign.

In contemplation there are no coincidences.

The next day the man who prayed was walking to the shops when he met an elderly woman who had lived in the area for many years. Without any prompting, she started to complain about all the trouble being caused by the young people. After a while, however, the tone of her voice changed and became much softer. She began to talk about the young man who, unbeknown to her, he had watched so intently the previous evening. She spoke about how he had once been such a lovely child who used to visit her home. But then his parent's marriage had broken up and his mother had had a succession of boyfriends. When they were around, the lad was not welcome at home. Now, the old lady said, she did not know the young man, but she remembered what he had once been. Shaking her head sadly, she walked away.

In contemplation there are moments when we glimpse the truth of how God sees us. In contemplation there are moments when we taste the love that God has for us.

14
Contemplation and truth

Contemplation requires a new relationship with language.

When we are not aware of being alive we confuse words with truth. We confuse a description with reality.

Words cannot ultimately be true. This means that thoughts can never be true, for words are just thoughts out-pictured into the world of form. Life is as it is, with nothing added and nothing taken away. Reality is what it is. Life can only be experienced. Thoughts and words are merely descriptions of reality. They can be wonderful, beautiful pointers to truth; they can evoke the experience of truth; and they can mirror the light of truth. Thoughts and words are necessary to help us open to the experience of truth. But they can never be truth itself. Thoughts and words, at best, can only be alarm clocks that wake us up to what was always present. They can be helpful or unhelpful, but never true.

We have needed to see words as truth in the past. Such an understanding of the nature of truth gave a wonderful anchor in a turbulent world and a framework for exploration. All of the great theologies and philosophies have been a beautiful blessing, but as a person moves increasingly into contemplative life a new understanding of the nature of truth is required. The words must become icons, through which we travel to limitless horizons.

On the contemplative path, slowly but surely, our anchor in the world becomes not our relationship with a set of ideas, but the nurturing of inner stillness and good fruit in the world. It is in this way that we discern the work of the Spirit. And the Spirit is not limited by our theologies and philosophies. It blows where it will and cannot be systematized. On the contemplative path we seek to be right, not consistent.

In contemplation, thoughts and words are only helpful when they relate directly to an individual's current mental world. Everyone needs something different. The difference may be great or small.

This can, however, create confusion.

I once heard a story about an abbot who was confronted by some of his monks.

"Holy Father," they exclaimed, "we have found you out! You have been tricking and misleading us. We demand an explanation and an apology."

"Oh yes," the abbot replied calmly, "and what is it that I am supposed to have done?"

"You know well what you have done," they exclaimed indignantly, "but let us explain in case it has slipped your mind. For years we have been your devoted students, coming to you with our problems and questions, believing that you were an enlightened, wise being who could lead us to God. But now we have found you out. We have been comparing notes and have discovered that you do not know what you are talking about. You have been separately giving us different, conflicting teachings. Two of us come to you separately with the same question, and you give us opposite answers. You have had a lot of fun at our expense, but now we've had enough."

The abbot sighed. "Let me explain what I see when I look at you. It is as though I am at the end of a long road, watching you come towards me. What I see is people who seem to be blind. Constantly wandering off the path in all directions. Always in danger of falling into ravines, colliding with trees, or tripping over. I see one of you veer to the right and I say 'move left' to get back on the path. Another goes off to the left, and I say 'move to your right' to regain the way. Then when you meet, the first says that to go to the left is the truth, whilst the second says, 'No, the truth is to the right!' Then you argue, maybe fight, perhaps try to force the other to go your way 'for the good of their soul', or you decide the teacher is a fraud."

The abbot paused and then spoke again. "You must understand that no teaching is the truth; each can only point towards the truth. The direction in which an individual will need to be led at a particular time will depend on the way they are facing. The truth is never a teaching; it is always an experience – the experience of God."

15

The rocky path of contemplation

To a mind that has been lost for a lifetime in the turmoil of thinking, the first taste of inner stillness is the sweetest thing.

A whole new world has been revealed. In the depths of daily practice, or the majesty of nature or in the mystery of another person's eyes, wonder and peace are discovered. The word "God" comes alive. We think we have arrived.

But we have not arrived. We have only just set out on the journey. We are walking gently through the lowlands and have yet to realize that, for some of the journey, there are steep climbs, uneven ground and bad weather ahead. When unexpected difficulties strike it is a great shock. The contemplative can quickly become demoralized. The first reaction is to think that something has gone wrong: it should not be this way and perhaps, even, God is to blame. There is a great temptation to turn back to the comfort of the valley. A contemplative has to learn not to turn back, but to face the challenges and discover that at the heart of each lies the God of truth. It is not uncommon for this lesson only to be learnt after a number of failures – and this is fine, for it is from our mistakes that we learn. Forgiveness of one's self is crucial in these times. Self-condemnation will only take one back into suffering. Guilt can be a form of avoidance.

More specifically, contemplative practice can lead to powerful experiences of fear and depression.

The world and a lifetime of conditioning insist that this is a bad thing and something has gone wrong. The Ancient Wisdom gently asserts that something is going very right. Though difficult, a great healing is occurring.

Such experiences are not unique to contemplation. They arise quite naturally in the lives of many people as a result of unconscious forces. In contemplation, however, such experiences arise through a conscious decision to face truth. They occur because in the stillness we have to face our minds. The difference is also that in contemplation the arising of fear and depression are seen as a great opportunity and challenge, to be faced and transcended, for they are symptoms of a mind that searches for the truth and rejects the false. Such experiences must be handled with great care, so that they do not become overwhelming. Experienced guides (whether in person or in writing) and spiritual community are vitally important at such times. If the experience does start to become overwhelming, it is time to return to the valley to rest and re-group.

Fear

Most of us have spent a lifetime and invested great energy in avoiding those parts of our minds where fearful thoughts lie. Fear can appear to be about the past, the future, or some experience we are having in the present. Actually, fearful thoughts are not so one-dimensional, but are multi-layered, pointing into the depths of consciousness. Such thoughts can take innumerable forms and, whether seemingly "big" or "small", appear to have terrible power. In truth, this power is an illusion. But we believe the illusion is real and take ourselves to another part of the mind and build great walls of manufactured mental activity, in which and behind which we hide. In doing so, we multiply exponentially the intensity of the illusion. God cannot get to us in our fantasies, for God is real. He will help us, however, to see the falsity in our minds – something for which it is easy to be ungrateful.

In stillness these walls begin to crumble and the fearful monsters that lie beyond are eventually glimpsed and remembered. This is the point where the contemplative path becomes rocky.

When such times come, we can be reluctant to acknowledge that we are afraid.

This can be because we know that to acknowledge the fear is to face it, and we feel we will be overwhelmed. This reluctance can also come from disappointment – we came to the spiritual path because of our struggles with life and it was meant to be the cure. It seems to have let us down. Or, there may be guilt involved. Perhaps we believe or have been taught that "spiritual" people are not supposed to be afraid – it is a sign of lack of faith, or we are meant to be beyond such things. Whatever the reason, the fear is denied and the longer it is denied the greater the power it accumulates. It is like a coiled spring gradually being pressed flat over time. It is better to allow release before it reaches its ultimate compression.

I had a profound experience with fear many years ago, when I was still new to the contemplative path. It taught me many things. One evening I had gone to listen to a lecture on the Christian healing ministry. At that point in my life I had not felt right for some time. An underlying, unexplained tension had become the general background to my daily life. Some time before that evening I had committed myself (and therefore also my family) to a financially very risky way of life, having convinced myself that, as I was doing "God's Will", the necessary funds would mysteriously arrive. They didn't, but I kept convincing myself that all was well and that I trusted God completely.

That evening, for reasons I do not understand, I saw through the lie. Suddenly and unexpectedly, the fear I had been suppressing broke through with tremendous power. In my mind, while the excellent speaker shared his wisdom unheard, I was shattered. The possible consequences for my family of what I had done filled my thoughts. I was also very angry with God. That evening not only did I learn that the contemplative path required honesty about fear, I also learned the tremendous healing to be found in talking to God with complete truth. I railed against God in my mind for the best part of an hour. I shouted, swore and reproached without inhibition. By the end of the evening, my mind was very still and the underlying tension had gone. I also felt very close to God. I heard very little of the talk on healing, but was blessed with its fruits.

Depression

I once saw a movie on the television. It was a western about Wyatt Earp, Doc Holliday and the gunfight at the O.K. Corral. Towards the end of the movie, Doc Holliday faced his arch rival, another gunslinger with whom he had crossed swords on numerous occasions. As they finally stood before each other, hands hovering over the butts of their guns ready to draw, the conversation between them became philosophical.

When a person is facing death this should not be unexpected. They mused briefly on why they both lived as they did. Lives filled with danger, killing, alcohol, gambling and uncommitted relationships. Then there was a pause and Doc's rival looked sad. "Really, you know, I live like this to fill the emptiness inside. It's like there's a big hole right at the center of who I am. And no matter how many fights, killings, booze and women I pour down that hole, it's still there. I can't stand it. I've spent my life running away from it. But wherever I go, it goes". Then he went for his gun, but Doc was too fast.

We all carry this void inside us, whether we are consciously aware of it or not. We are desperate to escape its pull, cover it over, and not have to look into the blackness. It is an absence of meaning. Without speaking, it shouts the question at us, "What is the point of anything?" We stand on the brink of the void when we are forced to acknowledge that everything and everyone dies. Our greatest achievements will always, eventually, fade. Those we love will one day, sooner or later, no longer be. We peer into the void when the daily struggles and monotony of life wear us down, and all that seems to lie ahead is more of the same until death comes. The vastness of space and time and our own seeming insignificance can easily make anything we do look pointless. The sense of powerlessness can be overwhelming. The mystery is terrifying.

So, like the gunslinger, each of us spends our life trying to cover the void. There are two basic strategies, usually mixed together.

The first is to use our imagination to create frenetic mental activity. We author, and believe with all our might, a great story as to what life is about. It might be a religious story. Or, it might be a story that says the purpose of life is the pursuit of pleasure, excitement, power, money, achievement, success, knowledge, tribal belonging, family or a special relationship. Usually, a number of these themes will be present. Each of these great themes will be lived out by different people in varying ways. For one person the pursuit of pleasure will involve a wild hedonistic lifestyle; for another, a day spent fishing. For some, tribal belonging will mean committing oneself to public service for the benefit of all or risking one's life in war. For others it will involve worshipping a football team. "Success" for a university graduate will be very different from that for a person less gifted.

We are the central character in our story, around whom everything and everybody else revolves. It is our stories that give us our sense of identity, and the identities that we project onto others and demand that they believe also. We seek out others who will share our belief in a particular story; who will enter into the conspiracy. We clash with others who believe a different story. Living out the stories creates vast, all-absorbing mental activity. We are too busy to give attention to the truth of life. Such stories are always time-bound. They are rooted in the past and point into the future. In fact, it is our stories that create much of our sense of time. When we are present now, the stories drop away.

There is nothing intrinsically wrong with such stories, as long as we do not confuse them with truth. Indeed, they give life a wonderful richness and joy. The measure is whether they are helpful or unhelpful. Some stories point beyond themselves to reality itself. They also become great vehicles for love, creation and growth. But they are only vehicles, to be discarded when no longer needed. At their best, this is the gift of religious stories. Stories are unhelpful when they point deeper into illusion and away from the experience of truth. They are unhelpful when they point to destruction rather than creation;

regression rather than growth. Strangely, religious stories are capable of this also. Whether a story is helpful or unhelpful will depend on where an individual is at a particular point in his life.

We live such stories with all that we have but, because they are ultimately not true, there will always be times when they no longer bring meaning. This is when it is difficult to get out of bed in the morning.

The second strategy which is adopted to cover the void is to dull the mind. This is the opposite of the first strategy, which is to create great, all-consuming activity in the mind. Through dulling consciousness, we hope to avoid awareness of the black hole of meaninglessness at the center of our lives. So, we dull consciousness with things like television, alcohol, drugs and, even, excessive sleep.

The two strategies are not mutually exclusive. Indeed, we spend our lives alternating between the two. Some of us give our energy to living our great story during the day, and then come home and vegetate with the television and a glass of whiskey. Others have given-up on their story and spend their day seeking the oblivion offered by various substances. Each of us has a shifting balance in our lives between these two strategies. When one seems to be failing, we reach for the other.

In contemplation, we let them both fail. In the stillness, we begin to see our stories for what they are and the void begins to beckon. Our meanings drop away. It can be a difficult time as life loses its taste. Interests, hobbies, ambitions drop away. We no longer know how to fill time. We long to go back to how we were. For some this is possible. For others, the journey back is closed – they are too committed to honesty.

Although we let these strategies fail, we do not do away

with stories for all time, for we need stories to live in the world. Rather, we let certain stories fail because we accept that these particular ones are no longer helpful. We rest on the edge of the void while new stories emerge which will be helpful; that will reflect more clearly the truth of existence. We let them fail so that in times to come we understand stories for what they are – not the truth, but pointers to the truth.

Walking the rocky path

When we encounter the rocky parts of the contemplative path there are two insights, or rather recollections that can help greatly.

First, we have to remember that we are not alone. At such times this can be very difficult to grasp, as we become even more self-absorbed than normal. We are suffering and our pain becomes the center of everything. The difficulty and the duration of the experience are thereby greatly amplified.

We are not alone because many others have walked this path before us and their wisdom is available in writing and, even better, in person. We are not alone because there are others walking the path now, with us, by our side. Spiritual community is one of the great refuges. But, more than anything else, we are not alone because a vast, limitless, loving intelligence is closer to us than the beating of our heart. In the Christian tradition we call this presence "God". As I discovered that evening in the healing lecture, through utter honesty on our part great healing is possible.

The second great recollection is so simple and obvious and it is easily missed. All things pass. The difficult parts of the path are just that – parts. The ground will level out again, the sun will shine and the birds will sing. But when we are struggling, it seems as though happiness has gone forever. To see the falsity of this belief can bring a great easing and, very often, even release. It is too easy to invent yet another story of who we are, but this time we are the suffering self, eternally doomed to hell. We have to see through this story as well.

In time, the rocky parts of the contemplative path become easier and easier. They are still encountered, but through experience we develop a new relationship with them. We cease to resist and start to appreciate. Our times of fear are seen as windows to see further into the depths of the mind and to lay old ghosts to rest. Our times on the edge of the void become full of meaning, but meaning that cannot be put into words. We begin to see the beauty of the void and to know that it is the truth of who we are.

Eventually, we understand that the contemplative path is not about feeling "good" or feeling "bad". It is about opening ourselves to live in truth, which is immeasurably deeper and more fulfilling than feeling either good or bad.

The Cosmic Christ

It is a late summer evening, just beginning to get dark. The sun is still to set on the western horizon, but is already lost behind a range of hills. The sky has been a beautiful clear blue all day, but is now darkening from the east. Soon there will be stars.

I stand on a cliff taking in the view. Below me, to the south, a calm sea gently breaks against the sand and stones of the beach. A sound heard for hundreds of millions of years – but only when there have been ears to hear.

The cliff face, which slopes away from me, reveals the ancient of days that is the Earth. The rock immediately below my feet is about one hundred million years old. But this is a thin layer, only a metre or so deep. Underneath can be seen much older deposits, up to two hundred million years old. And in this lower level is to be found abundant evidence of long-ago life. Countless fossils have been found here as the sea has done its work of erosion. And more – the bones and skeletons of dinosaurs are sometimes discovered. Life that has come and gone, each form totally absorbed in its own story.

As I feel the ancient land beneath my feet, I realize that my body is just the latest transient spark to occupy this space. In fact, every mineral, chemical compound and atom that believes it is "me" has been around since time immemorial. "I" have been rocks, plants, liquids, gasses and other living creatures since the start. And maybe "I" one day will be a fossil for sale in a shop. Strange creatures will "ooh" and "ah" at my imprint, before going to find an ice cream.

I am so temporary, so passing – is the universe even aware of me?

I am not alone on the cliff. My beloved is with me as always, in silence, as is often the case. I observe her for a while as the sky continues to darken. It hits me that the form I know so well will one day move, speak and keep silence no more. Not so long after that there will be just bone, and a little while later, perhaps, not even that. This should be shocking, but in this majestic, ancient setting nothing could seem more natural.

It is darker now and a few stars and a sliver of moon are emerging. The air is cooling after a hot day and my bare arms are starting to feel the chill.

As I stare at the sky it occurs to me that no matter how old the rocks I feel beneath my feet, compared to the cosmos above they have only just been born. My bones know in that moment that they are a part of something so awesome that words and thoughts fall away. It is only possible to absorb, and be absorbed by the moment, which is timeless.

In this place, in this moment, I realize that I do not know who or what I am. But there is a partial intuition of what I am for – to be there and to witness. I am the universe knowing itself. And so is every other conscious being. This insight brings with it a deep experience of love. It is the richest of moments. A life can never be the same again.

As the intensity of the moment fades a little, I turn and look inland. Many lights can now be seen and smoke rises from a couple of distant garden bonfires. About a mile away, a fun fair is in full swing and the amplified music can be faintly heard. A caravan park is directly below, full of intense, story-filled lives.

There was a time when I believed that the story of "my life" was all that I was. I revelled in the drama, the highs and lows, the plans and memories – not knowing of the wealth to be found on the cliff top. I did not know why I suffered.

Now I appreciate the story and acknowledge its importance. My story, and that of everyone else, is as much an expression of the cosmos as the cliff on which I stand and the stars at which I marvel. The human story must be lived fully. But it is not who I am or who we are. The mystery of who we are is to be found on the cliff top, looking outward and upward. It is unspeakable.

POSTSCRIPT

"At the present time there has been in the West a trend of feeling towards the contemplative aspect of prayer, and many have looked to Eastern religions for contemplative practice, partly as a result of the Church's sad neglect of its own contemplative tradition... It matters greatly for the renewal of the Christian Church that the contemplative vocation be more known and recovered."

MICHAEL RAMSEY
ARCHBISHOP OF CANTERBURY 1961-1974

FURTHER STUDY

Jesus said, "Know what is in front of your face, and what is hidden from you will be disclosed to you. For there is nothing hidden that will not be revealed."

A certain philosopher questioned the holy Anthony. "How," said he, "Dost thou content thyself, Father, who art denied the comfort of books?" He answered, "My book, philosopher, is the nature of created things, and as often as I have a mind to read the words of God, it is at my hand."

For further reflections on the contemplative
life and details of talks, seminars and retreats, visit
www.simonsmall.info

The Creative Christian
God and us; partners in creation

ADRIAN B. SMITH

Enlivening and stimulating, the author presents a new approach to Jesus and the Kingdom he spoke of, in the context of the evolution of our Universe. He reveals its meaning for us of the 21st century. – **Hans Schrenk**, *Lecturer in Holy Scripture and Biblical Languages, Middlesex University.*

9781905047758/1905047754•144pp £11.99 $24.95

The Gospel of Falling Down

MARK TOWNSEND

Humble, searching, faith-filled, and yet risky and creative at the same time. – Richard Rohr OFM

This little book is tackling one of the biggest and deepest questions which, unexpectedly, brings us to the foundation of the Christian faith. Mark has discovered this through his own experience of falling down, or failure.– **Bishop Stephen Verney**

9781846940095/1846940095•144pp £9.99 $16.95

I Still Haven't Found What I'm Looking For

PAUL WALKER

Traditional understandings of Christianity may not be credible but they can still speak to us in a different way. They point to something which we can still sense. Something we need in our lives. Something not just to make us decent, or responsible, but happy and fulfilled. **Paul Walker**, *former Times Preacher of the Year, rejoices in the search.*

9781905047765/1905047762•144pp £9.99 $16.95

The Way of Thomas
Nine insights for enlightened living from the secret sayings of Jesus

JOHN R. MABRY

What is the real story of early Christianity? Can we find a Jesus that is relevant as a spiritual guide for people today? These and many other questions are addressed in this popular presentation of the teachings of this mystical Christian text. Includes a reader-friendly version of the gospel.

9781846940309/1846940303•196pp £10.99 $19.95

You Are the Light
Rediscovering the Eastern Jesus

JOHN MARTIN SHAJANANDA 2nd printing

Closed systems, structures and beliefs have prevailed over the last 2000 years, cutting off the majority from direct contact with God and sharing Jesus's own insight on non-duality. This is an inspiring new contemplative vision. – *Scientific and Medical Network Review*

9781903816301/1903816300•224pp £9.99 $15.95

The Fall
The evidence for a Golden Age, 6,000 years of insanity, and the dawning of a new era

STEVE TAYLOR

The Fall is one of the most notable works of the first years of our century, and I am convinced it will be one of the most important books of the whole century.– **Elias Capriles**, *International Journal of Transpersonal Studies*

Important and fascinating, highly readable and enlightening. – **Eckhart Tolle**

9781905047208/1905047207•352pp £12.99 $24.95

The Trouble With God
Building the republic of heaven

DAVID BOULTON **Revised edition**

A wonderful repository of religious understanding and a liberal theologian's delight. – *Modern Believing*

Lively and stimulating, a crusading zeal imbued with both historical perspective and a bracing, unsentimental determination to assert that human spirituality, in all its fullness of transcendent potential, is sufficient to redeem us from the despair of nihilism and the banality of evil. – *Universalist*

9781905047062/1905047061•272pp £11.99 $24.95

O

is a symbol of the world,
of oneness and unity. O Books
explores the many paths of wholeness and spiritual understanding which
different traditions have developed down
the ages. It aims to bring this knowledge in
accessible form, to a general readership, pro-
viding practical spirituality to today's seekers.

For the full list of over 200 titles covering:

ACADEMIC/THEOLOGY • ANGELS • ASTROLOGY/
NUMEROLOGY • BIOGRAPHY/AUTOBIOGRAPHY
• BUDDHISM/ENLIGHTENMENT • BUSINESS/LEADERSHIP/
WISDOM • CELTIC/DRUID/PAGAN • CHANNELLING
• CHRISTIANITY; EARLY • CHRISTIANITY; TRADITIONAL
• CHRISTIANITY; PROGRESSIVE • CHRISTIANITY;
DEVOTIONAL • CHILDREN'S SPIRITUALITY • CHILDREN'S
BIBLE STORIES • CHILDREN'S BOARD/NOVELTY • CREATIVE
SPIRITUALITY • CURRENT AFFAIRS/RELIGIOUS • ECONOMY/
POLITICS/SUSTAINABILITY • ENVIRONMENT/EARTH
• FICTION • GODDESS/FEMININE • HEALTH/FITNESS
• HEALING/REIKI • HINDUISM/ADVAITA/VEDANTA
• HISTORY/ARCHAEOLOGY • HOLISTIC SPIRITUALITY
• INTERFAITH/ECUMENICAL • ISLAM/SUFISM
• JUDAISM/CHRISTIANITY • MEDITATION/PRAYER
• MYSTERY/PARANORMAL • MYSTICISM • MYTHS
• POETRY • RELATIONSHIPS/LOVE • RELIGION/
PHILOSOPHY • SCHOOL TITLES • SCIENCE/
RELIGION • SELF-HELP/PSYCHOLOGY
• SPIRITUAL SEARCH • WORLD
RELIGIONS/SCRIPTURES • YOGA

Please visit our website,
www.O-books.net